Identifying American Architecture

A Pictorial Guide to Styles and Terms 1600–1945

Second Edition, Revised and Enlarged

John J.-G. Blumenson

Foreword by
Sir Nikolaus Pevsner

With photographs from the
Historic American Buildings Survey

Commentary on the photographs by
David Harding Paine

AASLH

American Association for State and Local History
Nashville

First Edition 1977
Second Printing 1978
Third Printing 1979
Second Edition, revised and enlarged, 1981
Second Printing, Second Edition, February 1982
Third Printing, Second Edition, September 1982
Fourth Printing, Second Edition, November 1983
Fifth Printing, Second Edition, May 1984
Sixth Printing, Second Edition, May 1985
Seventh Printing, Second Edition, July 1986
Eighth Printing, Second Edition, August 1987
Ninth Printing, Second Edition, March 1989

Publication of this book was made possible in part by funds from the sale of the Bicentennial State Histories.

American Association for State and Local History
172 Second Avenue North
Nashville, Tennessee 37201

Library of Congress Cataloging-in-Publication Data

Blumenson, John J   G   1942-
  Identifying American architecture

   Bibliography: p. 117
   Includes index.
   1. Architecture—United States. 2. Architecture—United States—Terminology. I. Title.
NA7054.B55   1981   720'.973   80-28103
ISBN 0-910050-503 (pbk.)

Contents

Foreword

The Gothic style in Europe was the last totally original style for nearly four hundred years. Only the so-called International Modern of the early twentieth century was as independent of the past. The Renaissance depended on Imperial Rome. Baroque and Rococo admittedly used Renaissance and Imperial Rome with great originality. All the same the motifs were Revival, and for the nineteenth century the use of period precedent went so far as to make Historicism its all-pervading quality.

The situation in the United States was somewhat different. There was no Gothic and no Renaissance. The story of architecture begins with the Spanish Colonial on the West Coast and the English Colonial of New England and the East Coast. Neither of these two styles was a revival. They were the direct continuation of what had gone on (and was still going on) in Europe. And this direct contact had the consequence that as late as the Greek Revival of the early nineteenth century, one often could not recognize the county of origin of particular buildings, and the same can still be demonstrated for nearly the whole of Victorian Historicism.

The book which I am here attempting to introduce to you groups its short chapters differently. It begins with the Spanish Colonial but follows that immediately with what it calls the Mission Style, the Pueblo style, and the Spanish Colonial Revival. All three must be regarded as revivals of the original Spanish Colonial—revivals appearing as late as the late nineteenth and the early twentieth centuries.

The same situation is to be found on the East Coast. Here the Georgian-Palladian of England was directly continued. The dependence of American churches on Gibbs is a familiar topic. In the present book the treatment of Georgian Colonial, Federal, and Roman Classicism is continued by the treatment of what the book called Colonial Revival. Colonial Revival is of course what McKim, Mead & White stand for: a revival indeed, as the Spanish Colonial was. If you choose to call the Anglo-American Palladian a Palladian Revival, then McKim, Mead & White are a re-revival.

And yet another similar case: The neo-Italian Renaissance began in England about the 1830s, both as a Palazzo and a Villa Style (Barry being the leader in both fields). Our book has pages called Renaissance Revival and pages called Italian Villa, but immediately after them follows what is called Second Renaissance Revival. That of course refers to the other style pioneered by McKim, Mead & White, the style of the Boston Public Library and the Villard Houses in New York. If Barry's Renaissance was a revival, the Villard Houses are a re-revival.

These cases must suffice. I hope they have conveyed something of the method and the character of the book. To have over 200 illustrations and to have all of them reproduced from photographs will help the book to make its points.

However, it must be borne in mind that all value judgements are avoided. My attitude from the beginning would have been firmly to arrange the styles—and there are 39 of them—in the direction towards a climax, the climax being of course the achievement of the twentieth-century style, as the first style for cen-

turies in which period motifs were totally abandoned. I have in my writings always tried to measure the importance of an architect according to the originality of his style. This book does the opposite. All styles are evenly shown and evenly analyzed in their motifs. The method no doubt has considerable advantages. Starting from recognizing motifs you will soon recognize styles. Then, with the courage developed thereby, you will be capable of making your own value judgements; I need scarcely add that sound value judgements are essential, if in the end you want to plead for the preservation of the best. It should never be forgotten that to be fully armed for preservation battles is the supreme need, especially in America.

—SIR NIKOLAUS PEVSNER

Publishers' Preface
to the Second Edition

Three new features mark this second edition of *Identifying American Architecture*: for several styles discussed, additional photographs have been included; added commentary by Architectural Historian David Paine identifies the buildings pictured and points out specific characteristics that make these structures distinctive examples of the styles they typify; and the book appears, this time, in both hard cover and paperback, for those who have wanted to see it handsomely bound in a coffee-table, library edition, as well as those who love a sturdy, flexible, fit-in-your-pocket format. Our intention is to make this sound, down-to-earth guide indispensable to anyone who would like to study the marvelously varied architectural styles of America's buildings.

Preface to the First Edition

This handbook is intended primarily for the tourist or traveler to serve as a photographic guide to architectural styles and terms. The importance of the visual appreciation of architecture, which is the most visible of the arts, often is not apparent in the many excellent resources available. There are numerous books that document the history and development of architecture for the academician, dictionaries with descriptive definitions occasionally supported with line drawings for the student, and technical manuals providing specifications and information for architects, engineers and buildings conservationists. Histories, dictionaries, manuals and academic research are essential for a complete understanding of architecture; however many persons will agree with Hugh Morrison who wrote, ". . . in studying architecture we should learn to read buildings themselves, rather than mere words about them."

For the most part then, this handbook is aimed at the interested tourist or traveler, the high school and college student and the para-professional preservationist. The purpose of this brief guide is to provide photographic illustrations of buildings, architecture details, elements, and forms to enable the user to make visual associations and to begin to recognize styles and elements.

In order to give the reader as compact and easy to use handbook as possible, text is kept to a minimum and only exterior views of buildings are shown. Emphasis is on domestic architecture of an average nature rather than the well known house-museum, public and commercial building or monument. This will not preclude, however, the use of such examples in order to define clearly a particular style or term.

The handbook is divided into two parts. The first consists of styles and the second is a glossary of terms. Exception has been made to the normal historical chronological sequence of styles. Styles that have similar forms or characteristics follow one another. This visual organization is intended to simplify looking and comparing similar features, size, scale and other common elements. For example, the Colonial Revival style follows the Colonial styles of the seventeenth and eighteenth centuries. The brief description is followed by a list of characteristics and features keyed to the photographs illustrating each style.

The visual arrangement of architectural features is carried through into the glossary portion as much as possible. Representative views of the classical orders follow one and another as do doors, entrances, windows. It is also hoped that the index will provide easy reference for those seeking particular terms. For the sake of economy, it should be noted that within the limitations of this handbook, it has been impossible to include visual documentation of every known architectural term.

This handbook is sincerely presented to the reader as a first step toward a more complete understanding of architecture. The preparation of this handbook would have been impossible without the aid of many persons. In particular I wish to thank Gary Gore and his publication staff, Renee Friedman for her continuing support, and the staffs of the Historic American Building Survey, the National Register, and the National Trust for Historic Preservation for their cooperation and guidance in seeking the best available photographs.

A very special appreciation is extended to June Blumenson who in addition to spending hour upon hour typing the manuscript, provided invaluable advice and support throughout the project.

JOHN J.-G. BLUMENSON

Styles

Spanish Colonial   1600–1840

The Spanish Colonial house is characterized as a low, long one-story building with a covered porch extending along the facade. Adobe bricks or stone were used for wall construction. The wall often was covered with a lime wash or plaster. Extending roof beams and porch posts were left round or roughly squared. By the early nineteenth century, many two-story houses were built with encircling porches and covered with wooden shingles. The rear of the house often faced an enclosed patio or garden. Churches or missions of Texas and the Southwest were vernacular interpretations of contemporary Mexican church building in the Baroque style. They were richly ornamented with churrigueresque-style decoration or simplified Renaissance-style detailing.

1. Adobe brick with plaster finish
2. Roof beams or rafters (vigas)
3. Corredor (porch)
4. Rounded post with bracket-like capitals
5. Parapet wall
6. Canales (water spouts)
7. Shed roof
8. Clay tile
9. Enclosed patio
10. Hip roof with wood shingles
11. Two-tiered encircling porch
12. Curvilinear gable
13. Bell tower with saucer-like dome
14. Portal
15. Pilasters
16. Niche

A. Jose Maria Covarrubias Adobe, location unknown
B. Governor's House, Santa Fe, New Mexico
C. Mission San Luis Rey, near San Diego, California
D. Custom House, Monterey, California
The adobe walls and wide overhangs of these buildings demonstrate the Spanish Colonial builders' adaptation to climate and available materials in the American Southwest. The Mission San Luis Rey is a comparatively elaborate example of the vernacular adaptation of Mexican Baroque churches. Some mission churches were extremely simple adobe struc-tures, retaining only a few vestiges of Baroque church design.

Mission Style   1890–1920

Characteristic of the Mission style is simplicity of form. Round arches supported by piers punctuate stucco or plastered walls. Color and texture are provided in the broad red-tiled roof. Roof eaves with exposed rafters may extend well beyond the walls. At times the plain wall surface is continued upward forming a parapet. Towers, curvilinear gables and small balconies or balconets are used on large buildings. The only surface ornamentation is a plain string course that outlines arches, occasional gables and balconies.

1. Stucco or plaster finish
2. Arcades
3. Red-tiled roof surface
4. Curvilinear gable
5. Projecting eaves with exposed rafters
6. Canales (water spouts)
7. Coping or top of parapet covered with red tiles
8. Bell tower
9. Iron balconet
10. Archivolt trim
11. Piers
12. Impost molding

A. Santa Fe Railroad Station, San Diego, California
B. Alvarado Hotel, Albuquerque, New Mexico
C. Railroad Station, Burlingame, California
D. 2306 Massachusetts Avenue, Washington, D.C.
Mission Style is one of three revivals, at times difficult to distinguish from one another, all going back to Spanish Colonial precedents. These buildings employ recognizable features—the bell tower, for example—of Spanish missions to building programs—a railroad station—undreamed of in colonial times. The application of a stucco Mission Style facade to a Washington town house demonstrates how far revivalists could go to employ a fashionable style.

Pueblo Style   1905–1940

The Pueblo-style house is characterized by battered walls, rounded corners and flat roofs with projecting rounded roof beams or vigas. Straight-headed windows generally are set deep into the walls. Second and third floor levels are stepped or terraced, resembling the Indian habitats called pueblos of New Mexico and Arizona.

1. Flat roofs
2. Projecting roof rafters called vigas
3. Parapet wall with canales (water spouts)
4. Rounded corners
5. Battered walls
6. Unpainted round porch posts
7. Roughly hewn window lintels
8. Stepping or terracing

A. Fine Arts Building, Museum of New Mexico, Santa Fe, New Mexico
B. Santa Fe County Courthouse, Santa Fe, New Mexico
C. Southwest Region National Park Service Office, Santa Fe, New Mexico
The simple outlines, plain stucco walls, and projecting beams of these buildings are reminiscent of pueblo architecture, but also echo the simple vernacular adaptations of Spanish Colonial builders. The twin towers of the Fine Arts Building (A) closely resemble the very simple adobe mission churches built by Spanish priests in western outposts. This revival was largely confined to the American Southwest.

Spanish Colonial Revival 1915–1940

The unique feature of the Spanish Colonial Revival style is the ornate low-relief carvings highlighting arches, columns, window surrounds and cornices and parapets. Red-tiled hipped roofs and arcaded porches also are typical. Stone or brick exterior walls often are left exposed or finished in plaster or stucco. Windows can be either straight or arched. Iron window grilles and balconies also may be used. A molded or arcaded cornice highlights the eaves. The facades of large buildings often are enriched with curvilinear and decorated parapets, cornice window heads, and symbolic bell tower.

1. Enriched compound arch
2. Iron window grilles
3. Arcaded cornice
4. Arcades supported by columns
5. Carved and molded capitals
6. Molded cornice
7. Red tile roof
8. Enriched classical door surround
9. Enriched corbels
10. Curvilinear gable
11. Bell tower
12. Niches
13. Enriched cornice window head
14. Plastered and arched portal
15. Iron balconet
16. Arched window opening
17. Lintel-type window opening
18. Loggia

A. McAneeny Howerd House, Palm Beach, Florida
B. Nebraska Avenue, N.W., Washington, D.C.
C. Seaboard Coastline Railroad Station, West Palm Beach, Florida
D. Everglades Club, Palm Beach, Florida
E. Spanish Bungalow, Nashville, Tennessee

The buildings shown here, reminiscent of the grander, more obviously baroque examples of Spanish Colonial building, also demonstrate the style's popularity in Florida, which, like the Southwest, has a strong Spanish heritage. The vogue for revival of Spanish Colonial forms was not confined to the large-scale buildings in most of the preceding photographs. A stucco-walled, tile roofed variation in the modest bungalow was popular from 1913 through the 1920s all over the country.

E

A

B

C

New England Colonial   1600–1700

The New England house of the seventeenth century is characterized by a natural use of materials in a straightforward manner. The box-like appearance is relieved by a prominent chimney, a sparse distribution of small casement-type windows. The one-room house often was expanded by adding a room against the chimney end, forming a large house with a centrally located chimney. The well known "salt-box" shape house also provided rooms by extending the rear roof slope. Other useable space was made by placing windows in the gable end forming a half story. In larger houses the upper floor projected beyond the lower floors creating an overhang known as a jetty.

1. Centrally located large chimney
2. Gable roof
3. Riven or hand-split wooden shingles
4. Casement windows (See glossary)
5. Unpainted clapboards
6. Eaves close to wall
7. Vertical board and batten door
8. Extended rear slope of gable roof forming "salt box" roof
9. Pendants
10. Jetty or overhang
11. Corner post
12. Gable end Jetty or overhang

A. Jethro Coffin House, Nantucket Island, Massachusetts
B. Thomas Clemence House, Johnston, Rhode Island
C. Stanley Whitman House, Farmington, Connecticut
Building in the early years of the English colonies reflected the traditions of humble rural English building, contrasting with contemporaneous Spanish Colonial buildings based on grander, high-style Baroque architecture. Low ceilings, small windows, and rooms clustered around a central chimney reflect the builder's basic need to keep warm In the New England winter. The basic saltbox shape of such houses was often altered with a wing to the rear if the need for more room arose.

A

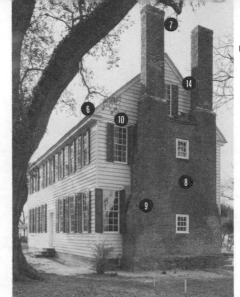

B

D

C

Southern Colonial   1600–1700

The Southern Colonial brick or timber frame house generally is narrow, only one room deep, and covered with a steeply pitched roof. Medieval characteristics such as curvilinear and stepped gables, massive chimneys, diagonal stacks, and a variety of brick bonds often are combined with classical elements, such as symmetrical arrangements of openings, modillioned cornices, and molded belt course.

A, D. Bacon's Castle, Surrey County, Virginia
B. Palmer Marsh House, Bath, North Carolina
C. Keeling House, Princess Anne County, Virginia
The need for less heat and more cooling ventilation is reflected in the planning of these buildings, frequently only one room deep, with chimneys on either end, with a passage through the center of the house. How different these buildings are from those now referred to by realtors as "Southern Colonial"—houses with some type of white columns and little if anything to tie them to Southern Colonial architecture.

1. Belt course
2. Narrow gabled projecting pavilion
3. Segmental relieving arch
4. Riven or handsplit shingles combed at ridge
5. Corbeled shoulder
6. Gable roof
7. Exterior chimneys
8. Chimney pent
9. Sloped weatherings
10. Narrow window openings
11. Diagonal stacks
12. Corbeled chimney caps
13. Flemish gable
14. Stacks rise separate from end wall
15. Flemish bond
16. Chevron pattern-bond
17. Modillion-like brackets along cornice
18. Water table

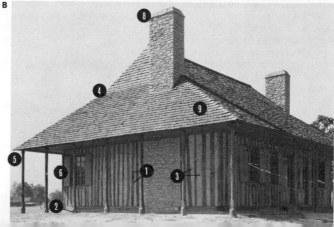

French Colonial   1700–1830

Early French settlers of the eighteenth century built structures of a half-timber frame method called post on sill or poteaux-sur-sole. The spaces between the vertical posts were filled with clay and rubble stone or sometimes bricks. The lower slope of the pavilion-type roof projects well beyond the walls, forming a cover for the porch or galerie. French-type double casement windows are hinged at the sides or jambs and latch at the center. In French plantation houses of the early nineteenth century, the main floor is raised and encircled by a covered galerie. An exterior staircase provides access to the main living quarters.

1. Posts
2. Sill
3. Rubble infill
4. Pavilion roof—a steep hip on hip type
5. Encircling porch or galerie covered by projecting roof slope
6. Double casement windows
7. Double doors with glazed panels (French window)
8. Large rubble stone chimneys
9. Riven or hand-split shingles
10. Small brick interior chimneys
11. Hip roof with flared eaves
12. Raised basement
13. Stuccoed brick columns
14. Thin wooden colonettes
15. Exterior staircase

A. Homeplace Plantation, Hahnville, Louisiana
B. Cahokia Courthouse, Cahokia, Illinois
Unlike the Spanish and English Colonial buildings pictured on preceding pages, with their strong ties to European roots, there is not much about these buildings that is especially French. They are well suited to the hot, damp climate where most, but obviously not all, French Colonial building took place, however.

A

B

D

C

Dutch Colonial   1700–1830

The early eighteenth century Dutch Colonial house built in brick or stone was covered by a steeply pitched gable roof. The straight-sided gables were finished with parapets raised on elbows. The most noticeable feature of the late eighteenth and early nineteenth century Dutch Colonial house is the gambrel roof. The lower slope of the roof often flared beyond the front and rear of the house forming a deep overhang.

1. Steeply pitched gable roof
2. Parapet wall
3. Elbows
4. Mouse-toothing or tumbling
5. Dutch cross bond
6. Iron anchor beams
7. Gambrel roof
8. ¼-round lights
9. Board and batten shutters
10. Gable with flared eaves
11. Wide horizontal boards
12. Stoop
13. Gable end chimney
14. Windows in gable or gambrel end

A. Wyckoff Homestead, Brooklyn, New York
B. Abraham Yates House, Schenectady, New York
C. Lefferts House, Brooklyn, New York
D. Van Nuyse (Ditmas) House, Brooklyn, New York
E. House, Nashville, Tennessee
The characteristic steep roof and wide overhangs were often combined with Georgian Style detail—the Lefferts House dormers, for example. Dutch Colonial style was revived in American suburbs of the early twentieth century, with varying degrees of fidelity to the prototype.

E

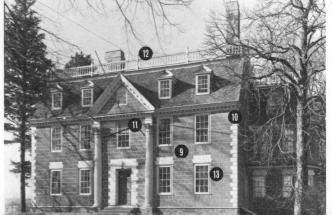

Georgian 1700–1800

The Georgian house is characterized by a formal arrangement of parts employing a symmetrical composition enriched with classical detail. The facade often is emphasized by a pedimented projecting pavilion with colossal pilasters or columns, and a Palladian or Venetian window. Sliding sash windows are common on houses of the eighteenth century. Each sash has several lights using as few as 6 or as many as 20 panes of glass in one sash.

A. Belmont Hall (Thomas Collins House), Smyrna, Delaware
B. Chase-Redfield House, Randolph Center, Vermont
C. The Lindens, Danvers, Massachusetts
D. Cliveden, Germantown, Pennsylvania

Relative prosperity and security brought to the English colonies buildings based on English precedents of a higher style than those of their early colonial predecessors. The rich and intricate ornamentation seen here stands in sharp contrast to the buildings pictured on pages 10 and 12. American Georgian church design displayed direct links to English churches of the time. St. Michael's Church, in Charleston, South Carolina, is one vivid reflection of the London churches of James Gibbs.

1. Coursed ashlar wall
2. Water table
3. Modillioned cornice
4. Belt course
5. Pedimented dormers
6. Urns on pedestals
7. Flat arch with pronounced keystone
8. Paneled door (see glossary)
9. Simulated ashlar finish
10. Quoins
11. Monumental columns
12. Balustrade on upper slope
13. Double hung sash windows (See glossary)
14. Pedimented entry
15. Fluted columns
16. Transom light
17. Monumental pilasters
18. Palladian or Venetian window
19. Side lights

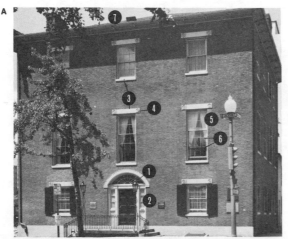

Federal   1780–1820

The Federal style is typified by a low pitched roof, smooth facade, large glazed areas and elliptical fan light with flanking slender side lights. Geometric forms such as polygonal or bowed bays accentuate the rhythm of the exterior as well as indicate new interior spaces. Tripart windows often are framed in recessed arches. Ornamental elements found on many of the houses during this period herald the work of the English designers, the Adam brothers.

1. Elliptical fan light
2. Side lights
3. Lintel-type window heads
4. Bull's eye corner block
5. Large lights
6. Thin muntins
7. Low pitch roof
8. Domed circular portico
9. Tripart windows in arched opening
10. Louvered shutters
11. Swags or garlands
12. Elliptical arch
13. Thin corner boards
14. Reduced architrave
15. Attenuated columns
16. Bowed bays
17. Smooth brick finish with fine joints

A. Decatur House, Washington, D.C.
B. Louisburg Square, Beacon Hill, Boston, Massachusetts
C. Meacham-Ainsworth House, Castleton, Vermont
D. Gore Place, Waltham, Massachusetts

Such elegant and intentional austerity as the Federal style of an antique American building is often surprising to twentieth-century eyes. The exterior austerity often cloaked a very decorated interior, in Adam Style, however.

Roman Classicism   1790–1830

Typical of Roman Classicism is the one-story Roman temple form employing variations of the Roman orders. The raised first floor is characteristic of design inspired by the proper Roman temple built on a platform or podium. The four-columned portico with pediment enclosing a lunette is one of the most often copied features in the Roman idiom which was popularized by Thomas Jefferson (1743–1826). Generally classical moldings are left plain without enrichment and painted white.

1. **Raised basement**
2. **Lunette**
3. **Plain entablature**
4. **Tail windows**
5. **Polygonal bay**
6. **Pedimented portico**
7. **Tympanum**
8. **Podium**
9. **Semi-circular fan light**
10. **Square plinth**
11. **Torus molding separated by scotia molding**
12. **Smooth shafts**
13. **Plain capitals**
14. **Smooth architrave**
15. **Bracketed projecting cornice**
16. **Arched window opening**
17. **Roman Orders (see glossary)**

A. Framington, Old John Speed Residence, Louisville, Kentucky
B. Ridgeway, St. Matthews, Kentucky
C. Old State Bank Building, Decatur, Alabama
This style is so closely linked with Thomas Jefferson that it is sometimes called Jeffersonian Classicism. Jefferson was a great admirer of Roman architecture, but also a follower of Palladio. The plan and massing of these houses, and of Jefferson's own house, Monticello, indicate a strong Palladian influence. Strong Roman influence is seen in the temple form of the Old State Bank. Jefferson's design for the Virginia state capitol grew out of his admiration for the Maison Carrée, an ancient Roman temple in Reims, France, and his design for the University of Virginia rotunda is an homage to the Pantheon in Rome.

24

Colonial Revival   1870–1920

The Colonial Revival house is often a combination of various Colonial styles and contemporary elements. Generally the Revival house is larger than its Colonial counterpart and some of the individual elements are exaggerated or out of proportion with other parts of the house. Historical details such as an eighteenth century swan's neck pediment or Flemish brick bond may be found on a house with large single-light window sash, stained glass, late nineteenth century bevel siding or large entry porches or porticos. Some Revival houses, however, are executed with such historical accuracy that they are difficult to distinguish from original houses.

A. Wilson House, Pittsburgh, Pennsylvania
B. Unidentified house, Manchester, New Hampshire
C. Stephen O. Metcalf House, Providence, Rhode Island
Window sashes (see A and B) and dormers (see B and C) are among the more obvious clues that these are revival buildings rather than the real thing, in spite of the high quality of all three designs. The Colonial Revival did not end altogether in 1920; it is still with us today, although the ability of present-day designers to employ historical forms with accuracy and/or finesse appears to be, with rare exceptions, drastically diminished.

1. Slate tile roof
2. Bevel siding
3. Swan's neck pediment (Different scale and shape)
4. Single-light sash
5. Large three-part window
6. Glass-paneled door
7. Oversize side lights
8. Square lights in upper sash
9. Single light in lower sash
10. Straight window heads
11. Large pilastered and arcaded chimney stack
12. Smooth brick finish in Flemish bond with fine joints
13. Brick end wall without chimney
14. Board siding on facade
15. Board siding on cheeks of oversize dormers
16. Shingle roof
17. Multiple upper-light sash with single-light lower sash
18. Bay window
19. Large balconied entry portico or porch
20. Louvered shutters on end wall

Greek Revival   1820–1860

The Greek Revival style is an adaptation of the classic Greek temple front employing details of either the Doric, Ionic, or Corinthian order. The columns support a full entablature and a low pitch pediment. Also many houses were built without the colossal temple front. The rectangular transom over the door was popular and often was broken by two engaged piers flanked by side lights that surround the door. The shouldered architrave trim was widely used for doors and windows. Upper floor lighting is incorporated ingeniously into the enlarged frieze of the entablature.

A. Joseph R. Jones House, Binghamton, New York
B. Andalusia, near Philadelphia, Pennsylvania
C. Louis Hammerschmidt House, Monticello, Illinois
D. Willard Carpenter House, Evansville, Indiana
E. Tennessee State Capitol, Nashville, Tennessee
Although the white-columned Southern plantation house is the popular idea of Greek Revival, the examples shown here help illustrate the style's national popularity. As mentioned earlier, white-columned houses, regardless of age or location, are often erroneously labeled "Southern Colonial." A house need not have a bank of white columns or a pedimented entry porch to qualify as Greek Revival. The pared-down simplicity of these buildings is typical of the Greek Revival aesthetic. Greek Revival was also employed in larger, nonresidential designs. It was ideal for state capitols in the young United States, when the idea of democracy still seemed to excite and motivate citizens and elected officials alike.

1. Doric Order
2. Pediment roof
3. Raking cornice
4. Tympanum
5. Ionic Order
6. Shouldered architrave trim
7. Tall first floor windows
8. Dentils
9. Entablature (architrave, frieze, cornice)
10. Attic story windows in frieze
11. Transom
12. Side lights
13. Corner lights
14. Pilaster corner boards
15. Return
16. Pediment-shaped window head

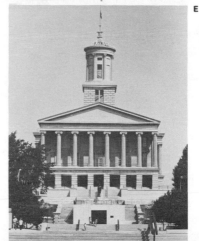

E

Egyptian Revival   1830–1850, 1920–1930

The Egyptian Revival style is identifiable by distinctive columns and smooth monolithic exterior finish. Characteristics are battered walls edged with roll or rope-like moldings, tall straight-headed windows with inclined jambs, and a deep cavetto or gorge-and-roll cornice. Generally roofs are flat and a smooth wall finish provides a monumental effect reminiscent of pylons or gateways to Egyptian temples. The later examples of Egyptian Revival used a cement or smooth ashlar finish to cover large buildings such as theaters.

1. Cavetto cornice
2. Battered walls
3. Roll or rope-like molding
4. Bundled shaft
5. Lotus flower capital
6. Random-coursed ashlar finish
7. Pylon tower
8. Sphinx
9. Smooth ashlar finish
10. Raven
11. Cavetto cornice window head
12. Vulture and sun disk symbol

A. Grove Street Cemetery Entrance, New Haven, Connecticut
B, C. Ada Theater, Boise, Idaho
Egyptian Revival style was one of the more exotic products of the nineteenth-century romantic turn of mind. Examples of it are found in widespread locations, although it was not frequently used. It seemed most appropriately applied to building projects associated with eternity and the afterlife—churches, prisons, or, as shown here, cemeteries. Egyptian Revival's potential for exotic, mysterious theatricality lent itself well to movie-palace design of the 1920s.

Gothic Revival   1830–1860

The popular Gothic Revival style was used for everything from picturesque timber cottages to stone castles. Characteristics of the Gothic cottage and villa are steeply pitched roofs, wall dormers, polygonal chimney pots, hood molds over the windows and a curvilinear gingerbread trim along the eaves and gable edges. The stone castle version of the style included a large carriage porch entry, large pointed windows with tracery and colored glass, towers, and battlements. The standard for Gothic Revival windows was variety. Church and civic architecture adapted Gothic principles and forms with more academic correctness. The exterior of many buildings was finished with vertical planks and strips in the board and batten technique.

A. Bowen House, Woodstock, Connecticut
B. James Winslow Gatehouse, Poughkeepsie, New York
C. St. Luke's Episcopal Church, near Cahaba, Alabama
D. Lyndhurst, Tarrytown, New York
Country cottages A and B are of the type popularized by the publications of Andrew Jackson Downing. There is little about them other than a pointed arch here and there to tie such designs to authentic Gothic building. Churches like St. Luke's (C), and similarly constructed houses, gave rise to the term *Carpenter Gothic*. Churches on a similar scale, constructed of stone, were often startlingly accurate copies of authentic rural English Gothic churches. Residential construction on such a scale as Lyndhurst shows was rare, limited, by necessity, to the few who could afford it. Churches on a larger scale were also built during the life of this style, Richard Upjohn's Trinity Church in New York being among the most celebrated.

1. Wall dormer
2. Oriel window
3. Bay window
4. Quatrefoil porch trim pattern
5. Hood mold with corbel stop
6. Wheel window
7. Polygonal chimney pots
8. Gingerbread vergeboard
9. Stucco finish
10. Slate roofs
11. Pointed arches
12. Carriage porch
13. Tracery window
14. Label mold
15. Tower with battlements
16. Lantern
17. Pinnacle with crockets
18. Tudor arch
19. Lancet windows
20. Corner buttress
21. Weatherings
22. Board and batten finish
23. Nave
24. Transept
25. Apse
26. Gable with crockets

Victorian Gothic   1860–1890

The most distinguishing feature of the Victorian Gothic style is the polychromatic exterior finish. Materials of differing colors and texture are juxtaposed, creating decorative bands highlighting corners, arches and arcades. Ornamental pressed bricks, terra cotta tile and incised carvings of foliated and geometric patterns also are used to decorate wall surfaces. Straight-headed openings are used in addition to traditional Gothic (pointed arch) windows and doors. In timber frame buildings the gable, porch, and eave trim is massive and strong, resembling the structural members. This is in sharp contrast to the lighter curvilinear gingerbread-type trim of the Gothic Revival.

A. Newburgh Savings Bank, Newburgh, New York
B. Chapel Hall, Gallaudet College, Washington, D.C.
C. Chancellor Green Library, Princeton University, Princeton, New Jersey
D. Converse House, Norwich, Connecticut
E. Christ Church, Nashville, Tennessee

This later, more free-wheeling interpretation of Gothic forms was well suited to the florid decorative approach of the late nineteenth century. Its use of heavy masonry and rich decorative and textural effects contrasts with the simplicity of the earlier revival of Gothic forms. Churches continued to be a mainstay of Gothic Revival, and, because the Gothic was so suitable for church design, the revival lingered on well into the twentieth century, long after it was no longer used for nonecclesiastical construction.

1. **Decorative stone bands**
2. **Stone quoins**
3. **Gothic (pointed arch) window opening**
4. **Lintel-type sash**
5. **Incised carvings**
6. **Relieving arch**
7. **Shouldered arch**
8. **Gabled entry**
9. **Hipped dormer**
10. **Cross gable**
11. **Corbeled turret with conical roof**
12. **Decorative brick bonds**
13. **Projecting pavilion**
14. **Equilaterial arch**
15. **Pressed brick and terra cotta tiles**
16. **Gable trim (see glossary)**
17. **Smooth horizontal board siding**
18. **Shed dormer**
19. **Balconet**
20. **Mitered arch window head**
21. **Polychromatic slate tiles**
22. **Cinquefoil arch**
23. **Trefoil arch**
24. **Polychromatic voussoirs**

E

Italian Villa   1830–1880

The outstanding feature of the Italian Villa style is the combination of the tall tower with a two-story "L" or "T" shaped floor plan. The roof with projecting eaves has a gentle pitch resembling the pediment shape of classical temples. Other distinctive features are the grouping of either straight or round-headed windows into threes or small arcades, and the placement of porches or arcaded loggias between the tower and house or at the corners. A smooth stucco finish highlights the classic simplicity of the design while an exuberance of enriched ornamentation provides a baroque appearance. The overall composition is an asymmetrical balancing of classical forms intending a picturesque quality.

1. Pediment or low-pitch roof gable
2. Large multiple scrolled brackets
3. Projecting eaves
4. Arcaded loggia
5. Lunette
6. Enriched modillion brackets
7. Rectangular bay
8. Vermiculated quoins
9. Segmental window heads
10. Enriched consoles
11. Triangular pedimented window heads
12. Low pitch gable roof
13. Balcony
14. Belt course

A. Morse-Libby House, Portland, Maine
B. J. P. Norton House, New Haven, Connecticut
C. Old Carlisle Home, near Marion, Alabama
While these examples are all rather imposing in scale, plans were published for more modest villas, though few were built. The tower is the feature that distinguishes the villa from the larger body of Italianate house designs, many of which are otherwise quite similar.

Italianate 1840–1880

The Italianate style is a rectangular (almost square), two or three-story house with very wide eaves usually supported by large brackets, tall thin first floor windows, and a low-pitch hip roof topped with a cupola. The formal balance of the house often is accentuated by pronounced moldings and details, such as string course and rusticated quoins. A central one-bay porch or long porches also are evident in the style.

1. Wide eaves
2. Large brackets
3. Tall first floor windows
4. Low pitch hip roof
5. Cupola
6. Double doors with glass panels
7. String course
8. Rusticated quoins
9. Stilted segmental window
10. Round arch
11. Hood mold or eyebrow window heads
12. Paired brackets
13. 2-light or pane sash
14. Enriched overdoor
15. Ancones

A. Brennan House, Louisville, Kentucky
B. James Dwight Dana House, New Haven, Connecticut
C. Willis Bristol House, New Haven, Connecticut
D. Moses Yale Beach House, Wallingford, Connecticut
E. Italianate Commercial Building, Nashville, Tennessee
Earmarks of the Italianate Style pictured here include the low roof pitch, bracketed cornice, round and segmental arched windows with decorative "eyebrows," recessed entry. These decorative features were applied to a huge variety of residential, commercial, and institutional buildings of all shapes and sizes. The three imposing houses at B, C, and D, square and rather formal, are not indicative of the huge range of the style. The Italianate commercial facade (E), interpreted in masonry, iron, or a combination of the two, appeared downtown in nearly every American city, large or small.

E

Renaissance Revival 1840–1890

Buildings in the Renaissance Revival style show a definite studied formalism. The tightly contained cube is a symmetrical composition of early sixteenth century Italian elements. Characteristics include finely cut ashlar that may be accentuated with rusticated quoins, architrave framed windows, and doors supporting entablatures or pediments. Each sash may have several lights or just one. A belt or string course may divide the ground or first floor from the upper floors. Smaller square windows indicate the top or upper story.

1. Smooth ashlar finish
2. Belt course
3. Pedimented window heads
4. Rusticated quoins
5. Entry framed by pilasters supporting a full entablature
6. Cornice window head
7. Architrave window frames
8. Multilight window sash
9. Architrave cornice
10. Segmental window heads supported with ancones
11. Paneled apron
12. Paneled pilasters
13. Molded window sill supported by corbels
14. Balustrade above cornice

A. Tully Bowen House, Providence, Rhode Island
B. India House, New York, New York
C. United States Post Office, Georgetown, Washington, D.C.
The relative faithfulness to Italian Renaissance precedents of window and portal treatments immediately distinguish this style from the much looser adaptations of the Italianate style.

The Second Renaissance Revival   1890–1920

Scale and size distinguish the later Revival from the earlier Renaissance Revival. Large buildings—usually three tall stories—are organized into distinct horizontal divisions by pronounced belt or string courses. Each floor is articulated differently. If the Doric Order or rustication is used on the first floor then the upper floor will be treated with a different order and finish. The window trim or surround also usually changes from floor to floor. Additional floors are seen in the small mezzanine or entresol windows. Arcades and arched openings often are seen in the same building with straight-headed or pedimented openings. Enriched and projecting cornices are supported with large modillions or consoles. The roof often is highlighted with a balustrade.

1. Rusticated ground floor
2. Stucco second floor
3. Molded belt course
4. Small fourth floor or attic story windows
5. Enlarged belt course to include frieze and cornice
6. Main cornice
7. Single-light sash
8. Arcaded and rusticated ground level
9. Monumental arcaded recessed gallery
10. Rusticated stone quoins
11. Entresol windows
12. Balustrade
13. Modillions and dentils

A. Racquet and Tennis Club, New York, New York
B. John Wilkins Residence, Washington, D.C.
In turning to larger Renaissance buildings for models, architects working in this style opened the door for greater size, textural richness, and variety in form. The style well suited the grandiosity required by a very rich client like Cornelius Vanderbilt, who commissioned The Breakers, in Newport, Rhode Island.

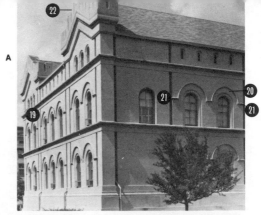

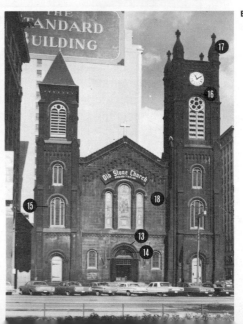

Romanesque Revival   1840–1900

The monochromatic brick or stone Romanesque Revival building is highlighted by the semi-circular arch for window and door openings. The arch is used decoratively to enrich corbel tables along the eaves and belt or string courses marking horizontal divisions. The archivolt or intrados of compound arches and the capitals of columns are carved with geometric medieval moldings. Facades are flanked by square or polygonal towers of differing heights and covered with various roof shapes.

A. General Land Office Building, Austin, Texas
B. First Presbyterian Church, Cleveland, Ohio
C, D. First Presbyterian Church, Galveston, Texas
Church design saw the most frequent application of this style, which, like the Gothic Revival, also based on medieval building, was ideally suited to the purpose. Secular buildings in the style were usually large governmental or institutional buildings, rather than dwellings.

1. Gabled nave
2. Blind arcade
3. Gabled tower
4. Tower with pyramidal roof
5. Wall buttress
6. Gablet
7. Corbel table
8. Splayed window opening
9. Corner buttress with obelisk-like pinnacle
10. Spandrel
11. Pier
12. Archivolt
13. Compound arch
14. Tympanum
15. Hood mold with corbel stop
16. Tower with parapets
17. Domed corner buttresses
18. Monochromatic stone finish
19. Round arched openings
20. Pronounced archivolt trim
21. Molded impost course
22. Battlemented parapet

Victorian Romanesque   1870–1890

A polychromatic exterior finish combined with the semi-circular arch highlight the Victorian Romanesque style. Different colored and textured stone or brick for window trim, arches, quoins and belt courses relieve the rock-faced stone finish. Decorated bricks and terra cotta tiles in conjunction with stone trim also may be used. The round arches usually are supported by short polished stone columns. Foliated forms, grotesques, and arabesques decorate capitals, corbels, belt courses and arches. Windows vary in size and shape.

A. Riley Row, Nina and Laurel streets, St. Paul, Minnesota
B. Slater Memorial Museum, Norwich, Connecticut
C. University of Texas Medical School Building, Galveston, Texas
D. Alexander Hall, Princeton University, Princeton, New Jersey
Like Victorian Gothic compared to the Gothic Revival, Victorian Romanesque was a freer interpretation of historical forms, visually heavier and more ornate than Romanesque Revival. It was also more readily adaptable to all types of construction, residential included, provided the scale was large enough to employ the characteristic heavy stonework.

1. Semi-circular arched openings (see glossary)
2. Short columns
3. Tower with conical roof
4. Steeply pitched gabled dormer
5. Checkerboard stone work
6. Corbel table
7. Transomed windows
8. Brick finish with rock-faced stone trim
9. Decorative stone bands and patterns
10. Niche with canopy in spandrel of arch
11. Foliated capital
12. Polished stone columns
13. Rock-faced coursed ashlar
14. Arcaded attic story
15. Monumental pilastered arcades
16. Projecting gabled pavilion
17. Rounded buttress
18. Polychromatic voussoirs
19. Curvilinear parapet wall
20. Gabled porch with compound round arched entry

A

B

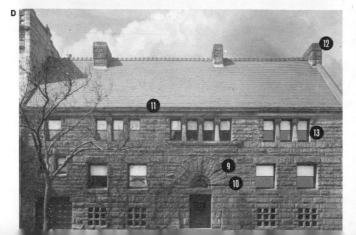

D

C

Richardsonian Romanesque 1870–1900

Richardsonian Romanesque houses, following the examples of H. H. Richardson (1838–1886), are characterized by a straightforward treatment of stone, broad roof planes and a select distribution of openings. The overall effect depends on mass, volume, and scale rather than enriched or decorative detailing. The uniform rock-faced exterior finish is highlighted with an occasional enrichment of foliated forms on capitals or belt course. The facade is punctuated with transomed windows set deeply into the wall and arranged in groups in a ribbon-like fashion. The large arched entry without columns or piers for support is the one most often used. Towers are short and chimneys are usually squat so as not to distract from the solid shape of the building.

1. Broad hip roof with cross gables
2. Smooth piers with enriched capitals
3. Short towers
4. Segmental arched entry
5. Transomed windows arranged in ribbon-like fashion
6. Round arched entry with return at impost level
7. Rock-faced coursed ashlar finish
8. Decorative flashing ridge
9. Relieving round arch
10. Carved tympanum
11. Eaves close to wall
12. Short and squat chimneys
13. Deep-set windows
14. Large hip roof with flared eaves
15. Brackets
16. Corbels
17. Broad round arch without columns
18. Hip roll

A. Old Chicago Historical Society, Chicago, Illinois
B, D. John J. Glessner House, Chicago, Illinois
C. Old Colony Railroad Station, North Easton, Massachusetts
Richardson's unique ability to deal with stone and mass and his frequent avoidance of carved and/or applied ornament (B and D) set him apart. Few could or did follow his lead, but his designs had a well-documented effect on Louis Sullivan.

The Octagon   1850–1860

The octagon was an innovation in American domestic architecture. The concept of the centrally planned home was far advanced of the time. The ideal octagon was a two- to three-story house characterized by a raised basement, encircling verandas or porches, a cupola, belvedere or roof deck, and minimal ornamental detailings. According to Orson Fowler (1809–1887) the inventor of the octagon house, the beauty of the house rests with its forms, the economy of materials (concrete), the functional interior, and the splendid views offered by any one of eight exposures in addition to observations from the roof. Fowler conceived of the octagon house from rethinking the needs and requirements of the working-class family. The octagon house was accepted across the country and adapted to various styles.

1. Encircling veranda or porch
2. Domical roof
3. Cupola
4. Decorative half timber
5. Scored concrete walls
6. Raised basement
7. Low pitch roof
8. Bell-cast porch roof
9. Cornice with dentils

A. Armour-Steiner House, Irvington-on-Hudson, New York
B. Alonzo Benedict House, Prairie du Chien, Wisconsin
C. Rich House, Akron, New York
Orson Fowler may have intended octagons to be minimally decorated, but as the Armour-Steiner House shows, ever-decorative Victorians didn't always listen. Perhaps the largest and most exotic octagon ever built—or, in this case, half-built—was Haller Nutt's Longwood, in Natchez, Mississippi. The structure was also known as Nutt's Folly.

A

B

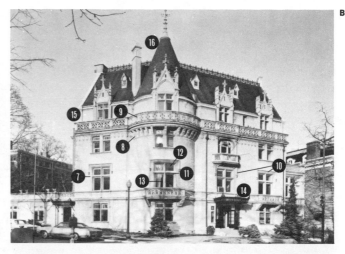

C

Chateau 1860–1890

The Chateau style is massive and irregular in silhouette. It is characterized by steeply pitched hip or gable roofs with dormers, towers, and tall elaborately decorated chimneys with corbeled caps. Croisettes or cross windows are paired and divided by a mullion and a transom bar. The basket-handle arch, similar to a Tudor arch without a point, also is used for windows. At times Renaissance elements such as semi-circular arches or pilasters are mixed with hood molds, Tudor arches, stone window tracery, and finials of the Gothic style.

A. Kimball House, Chicago, Illinois
B. 2349 Massachusetts Avenue, N.W., Washington, D.C.
C. Chalet Schell, Northfield, Massachusetts
The stone construction and large scale demanded by this style made it the exclusive province of wealthier clients, most of whom wanted impressive residences.

1. Truncated hip roof
2. Roof cresting
3. Cross gable with low-relief sculpture in gable
4. Tall chimneys with decorated caps
5. Hip knob with finial
6. Renaissance style entry with semi-circular arch
7. Croisette or cross window
8. Corbeled cornice supporting a continuous balcony
9. Quatrefoil and arched tracery
10. Label mold
11. Transom bar
12. Transom
13. Mullion
14. Canopy
15. Attic story
16. Tower with conical roof
17. Basket-handle arch
18. Hood mold with ogee arch trim
19. Window tracery
20. Balustraded terrace

Second Empire   1860–1890

The Second Empire style house is an imposing two or three-story symmetrical square block with a projecting central pavilion often extending above the rest of the house. The distinguishing feature is the mansard roof covered with multi-colored slates or tinplates. Classical moldings and details such as quoins, cornices, and belt course have great depth and are dramatized by different textures and colored materials. Windows are arched and pedimented, sometimes in pairs with molded surrounds. Entrance doors often are arched double doors with glass upper panels. First floor windows are usually very tall.

1. Mansard roof with straight sides
2. Gallery
3. Roof cresting
4. Bracketed cornice
5. Central pavilion
6. Paired windows
7. Mansard roof with convex sides
8. Multi-colored and patterned slate tiles
9. Metal curbs
10. Arched double doors with glass panels
11. Belt course
12. Veranda-like porch
13. Porthole dormer
14. Tall chimney with decorated caps
15. Paired brackets supporting eaves
16. Stone quoins with brick finish
17. Mansard roof with concave sides
18. Tall first floor windows
19. Eyebrow-like window heads
20. Paneled frieze boards

A. 201 Union Street, Schenectady, New York
B. John Jackson House, Petersburg, Virginia
C. Maplewood, Fairfax, Virginia
D. David Davis Mansion, Bloomington, Illinois
E. Executive Office Building, Washington, D.C.
Deriving its name from the French Second Empire, this style is set apart by the use of the mansard roof, long characteristic in French building. Beneath the mansard roof, examples of the style frequently resemble Italianate and Italian Villa designs quite closely. The style was also employed in a number of large civic, state, and federal buildings, echoing the scale and spirit of the public works undertaken in France under Napolean III.

E

Eastern Stick Style   1860–1890

The asymmetrical composition of the Eastern Stick style is highlighted by functional-appearing decorative "stick work". Steeply pitched gable roof, cross gables, towers and pointed dormers, and large verandas and porches are also characteristic. The resulting pattern of vertical, horizontal and diagonal boards applied over the horizontal siding becomes highly decorative. Oversized and unornamented structural corner posts, roof rafters, purlins, brackets, porch posts and railings complement the decorative "stick work". Sash or casement-type windows have either single or multiple lights.

1. Projecting gable
2. Diagonal braces
3. Horizontal siding
4. Purlins
5. Porch rafters
6. Corner posts
7. X braces
8. Projecting bay
9. Sill
10. Struts or diagonal brackets
11. Studs
12. Knee brace
13. Pendant

A, B. John N. A. Griswold House, Newport, Rhode Island
Although much of the stick work was decorative, it was meant to express honestly the structural character of the house. Eastern Stick detailing often resembles the early Gothic Revival, while scale and massing are much like that of the contemporaneous Queen Anne Style.

Western Stick Style   1890–1920

The open and informal Western Stick style house is characterized by gently pitched gable roof that spreads out well beyond the walls and projecting balconies, porches, recessed entries, and attached loggias. A unique feature of the style is the attenuated and exposed stick-like roof rafters and purlins that project well beyond the ends of the roof. Window lintels, railings and other beams protrude through vertical posts. When pegs are used to join the horizontal and vertical members, the ends are rounded and polished as are the corners of posts, beams and rafters. The exterior finish of wood shingles or wood siding is protected by earth-tone stains.

1. **Gently pitched gable roofs**
2. **Projecting balcony**
3. **Projecting second story porch**
4. **Exposed and extended rafters with attenuated ends**
5. **Projecting purlins**
6. **Window sill**
7. **Extended balcony sill**
8. **Protruding balcony rail**
9. **Casement-type window**
10. **Shingle siding**

A. Gamble House (Greene and Greene Library), Pasadena, California
As its name indicates, this style was largely a West Coast phenomenon, though ideas behind designs like the Gamble House were echoed on a smaller, much less expensive scale in many of the thousands of bungalows built all across the country from 1900 through the 1920s. The low roof pitch, wide overhangs, exposed rafters, generous porches, and shingle siding seen here were all part of the prototypical bungalow look, though countless variations followed.

Eastlake   1870–1890

Eastlake was a popular decorative style of ornamentation found on houses of various other styles, e.g. Victorian Gothic, Stick Style and Queen Anne. This decorative style is named for Charles Locke Eastlake (1833–1906), an English interior designer and critic of Gothic Revival style. Porch posts, railings, balusters and pendants were characterized by a massive and robust quality. These members were worked or turned on a mechanical lathe, giving the appearance of heavy legged furniture of the period. Large curved brackets, scrolls and other stylized elements often are placed at every corner, turn or projection along the facade. Perforated gables and pediments, carved panels, and a profusion of spindles and lattice work found along porch eaves add to the complexity of the facade. These lighter elements combined with the heavier and oversized architectural members exaggerated the three-dimensional quality.

1. Tapered round posts
2. Spindle and spool-like balusters
3. Spindles along porch frieze
4. Carved panels
5. Round porch posts
6. Fan-like brackets
7. Lattice-like porch base
8. Cutout pattern between porch balusters
9. Massive turned posts with knobs
10. Moldings
11. Scroll brackets

A. Old San Diego House, now destroyed
B. Moses Grinter House, Muncie, Kansas
C. Long-Waterman House, San Diego, California
Although these examples are in the Queen Anne Style, with Eastlake porches, entire houses can be termed Eastlake, as well. They are similar in over-all effect to both the Eastern Stick and the Queen Anne styles, but are generally smaller in scale.

A

B

Shingle Style 1880–1900

The Shingle style house, two or three stories tall, is typified by the uniform covering of wood shingles (unpainted) from roof to foundation walls. The sweep of the roof may continue to the first floor level providing cover for porches, or is steeply pitched and multi-planed. The eaves of the roof are close to the walls so as not to distract from the homogeneous and monochromatic shingle covering. Casement and sash windows are generally small, may have many lights, and often are grouped into twos or threes.

1. Gable roof with long slopes
2. Multi-light casement windows
3. Shingle siding
4. Shingle-covered porch posts
5. Two story bays
6. Pent roof
7. Eaves close to the wall
8. Multi-gabled roof
9. Circular two-tiered porch
10. One-story gabled porch
11. Multi-light sash windows
12. Undulating or wave-pattern shingle siding
13. Conical roofed tower with hip knob and finial
14. Gable end pent

A. William G. Low House, Bristol, Rhode Island, now destroyed
B. Isaac Bell House, Newport, Rhode Island
Developed in New England before spreading to the rest of the country, this style has been seen as a revival of early New England Colonial forms. The rambling plan, irregular massing, and ample verandas are reminiscent of other late-nineteenth-century styles, but the Shingle Style's lack of applied fancy-work stands in contrast to the others. H. H. Richardson and McKim, Meade, and White were responsible for some of the most celebrated of the Shingle Style designs, and Frank Lloyd Wright's earliest work was often Shingle Style.

Queen Anne Style   1880–1900

The Queen Anne style is a most varied and decoratively rich style. The asymmetrical composition consists of a variety of forms, textures, materials and colors. Architectural parts include towers, turrets, tall chimneys, projecting pavilions, porches, bays and encircling verandahs. The textured wall surfaces occasionally are complemented by colored glass panels in the windows. Elements and forms from many styles are manipulated into an exuberant visual display.

A. Long-Waterman House, San Diego, California
B. Haas-Lilienthal House, San Francisco, California
C. Old San Diego House, now destroyed
This style as manifested in America has little if anything to do with the architecture of the English Queen's time. It is the first thing that comes to many peoples' minds when a "Victorian mansion" is mentioned. Although Queen Anne houses often employed elaborate woodwork of the Eastlake type, the style also made creative, decorative use of a host of other materials, including masonry (the chimney in the old San Diego house, for example) and occasional touches of classical motifs, like the swan-neck pediment and swags on the Haas-Lilienthal House.

1. Tower with conical roof
2. Multi-planed roof
3. Projecting attic gable with recessed porch
4. Pedimented and projecting dormer
5. Fish scale shingles
6. Upper sash with a border of small square lights
7. Horizontal siding
8. Swags
9. Board and batten
10. Roof cresting
11. Eyelid dormer
12. Domed turret with recessed porch
13. Stained glass transom
14. Flared second story with shingle siding
15. Finial
16. Pendant
17. Verge boards
18. Circular bay
19. Variant of Palladian window
20. Tall thin chimney with terra cotta panels
21. Diagonal pattern shingles
22. Polygonal turret with tent roof
23. Carved wood panels
24. Encircling porch or verandah
25. Multi-gabled roof

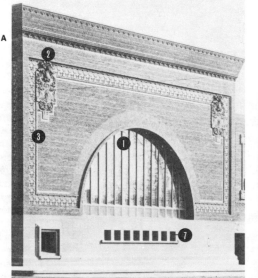

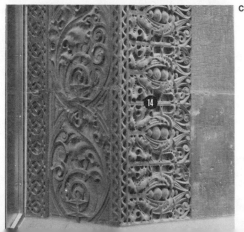

Sullivanesque   1890–1920

An intricate weaving of linear and geometric forms with stylized foliage in a symmetrical pattern is the unique element of the Sullivanesque style, originated by Louis Sullivan (1856-1924). Bold geometric facades are pierced with either arched or lintel-type openings. The wall surface is highlighted with extensive low-relief sculptural ornamentation in terra cotta. Buildings often are topped with deep projecting eaves and flat roofs. The multi-story office complex is highly regimented into specific zones—ground story, intermediate floors, and the attic or roof. The intermediate floors are arranged in vertical bands.

1. Large arched window
2. Decorative terra cotta panel
3. Decorative band
4. Vertical strips of windows
5. Pilaster-like mullions
6. Projecting eaves
7. Lintel-type opening
8. Highly decorated frieze
9. Enriched foliated rinceau
10. Porthole windows
11. Decorated terra cotta spandrels
12. Capital of pilaster strips
13. Guilloche enrichment
14. Foliated and linear enrichments along jambs or entry

A. National Farmer's Bank, Owatonna, Minnesota
B, C, D. Wainwright Building, St. Louis, Missouri
Sullivan's complex, often murky theorizing and his singular genius with ornament created a personal style that had few imitators or followers. However, Sullivan is one of the few human beings to whom Frank Lloyd Wright publicly acknowledged a debt of influence in his career.

Beaux Arts Classicism 1890–1920

Beaux Arts Classicism is characterized by large and grandiose compositions with an exuberance of detail and variety of stone finishes. Highlights of the style are projecting facades or pavilions with colossal columns often grouped in pairs, enriched moldings and free-standing statuary. Windows may be enframed by free-standing columns, balustraded sill, and pedimented entablature on top. Pronounced cornices and enriched entablatures are topped with a tall parapet, balustrade, or attic story.

1. Pedimented central pavilion
2. Monumental coupled columns
3. Aedicula or tabernacle window enframement
4. Balustrade
5. Pedestal with rusticated ashlar finish
6. Enriched cornice with rinceau frieze
7. Statuary
8. Pilastered parapet with sculptured rondelles or medallions
9. Sculptured spandrels
10. Attic story
11. Rusticated raised basement and ground story
12. Caryatides and atlantes

A. Union Station, Columbus, Ohio, now destroyed
B. Indiana National Bank Building, Indianapolis, Indiana
C. District Building, Washington, D.C.
The style takes its name from the École des Beaux-Arts in Paris, where some of America's most prominent turn-of-the-century architects had studied. Its grandiose use of classical forms was employed to great popular success at the World's Columbian Exposition in Chicago in 1893 and became an ideal medium to express corporate wealth (Indiana National Bank) or civic pride (District Building).

Neo-Classicism   1900–1920

Neo-classicism is based on primarily the Greek and to a lesser extent the Roman architectural orders. It is distinguished by symmetrically arranged buildings of monumental proportions finished with a smooth or polished stone surface. Colossal pedimented porticos may highlight the facade flanked by a series of colossal pilasters. When windows are employed they are large single-light sashes. Attic stories and parapets are popular but statuary along the roof lines is never employed. Since the Greek Orders are preferred, the arch is not often used and enriched moldings are rare.

1. Colossal portico in Ionic Order
2. Attic story
3. Unenriched entablature
4. Large single-light sash
5. Parapet
6. Pilasters
7. Unadorned roof line
8. Smooth ashlar finish
9. Roman Doric colossal columns

D

A. Lillian L. Massey Building, University of Toronto, Toronto, Ontario, Canada
B. Union Station, Toronto, Ontario, Canada
C. Canada Customs Building, Bay and Front streets, Toronto, Ontario, Canada
D. Small neo-classical house, Nashville, Tennessee

Calmer and less theatrical than Beaux Arts, Neo-Classicism reflects the prevailing vogue for classical forms in the first decades of the twentieth century. This was not a strictly Canadian phenomenon, as these examples might indicate, but was common all over North America. In addition to its use in massive buildings requiring a grand scale, the Neo-Classic style is in evidence in middle-class houses all across the country.

Bungalow Style   1890–1940

The typical bungalow is a one-story house with gently pitched broad gables. A lower gable usually covers an open or screened porch and a larger gable covers the main portion of the house. In larger bungalows the gable is steeper, with intersecting cross gable or dormers. Rafters, ridge beams and purlins extend beyond the wall and roof. Chimneys are of rubble, cobblestone or rough-faced brick. Porch piers often are battered. Wood shingles are the favorite exterior finish although many use stucco or brick. Exposed structural members and trim work usually are painted but the shingles are left in a natural state or treated with earth-tone stains. Windows are either sash or casement with many lights or single panes of glass. Shingled porch railings often terminate with a flared base. The bungalow, like other simple but functional houses, was subject to variations such as the California, the Swiss, the Colonial, Tudor and others according to locale and fashions of the time.

A. Unidentified bungalow house, Washington, D.C.
B, C. Bungalow house, Linsmore Crescent, Toronto, Ontario, Canada
D. Bungalow, Nashville, Tennessee
The bungalow had roots, like the Western Stick Style, in the Craftsman movement, but took on a life of its own and outlived them both. An American classic, bungalows were built by the thousand all over the continent in a huge variety of configurations and exterior finishes. The bungalow began to give way in the 1920s to modest houses in specific revival styles, like Spanish Colonial or English Tudor, and finally expired in the depression.

1. **Gabled roof facing the street**
2. **Shed dormer**
3. **Wood shingle siding**
4. **Tapered porch posts**
5. **King post**
6. **Tie beam**
7. **Rafters**
8. **Wall plate**
9. **Collar beam**
10. **Knee braces**
11. **Wide window opening**
12. **Battered porch piers**
13. **Flared base**
14. **Sun porch**
15. **Exterior chimney**
16. **Small windows flanking chimney**

Prairie Style   1900–1920

The Prairie style consists of a one- or two-story house built with brick or timber covered with stucco. The central portion rises slightly higher than the flanking wings. The eaves of the low-pitch roof extend well beyond the wall creating a definite horizontal and low to the ground quality. The large and very low chimney is found at the axis of the intersecting roof planes. Extending walls form the sides of terraces, balconies or delineate walks and entrances. Casement windows grouped into horizontal bands and sometimes continuing around corners emphasize the length of the house. The exterior walls are highlighted by dark wood strips against a lighter stucco finish or by a coping or ledge of smooth stucco along brick walls.

1. Low-pitch hip roof with projecting eaves
2. Brick wall with stucco ledge or coping
3. Raised central block or anchor
4. Brick finish
5. Terraces
6. Balcony
7. Gabled roof with horizontal projecting eaves
8. Chimney at intersection of roof planes
9. Stucco finish
10. Dark wood bands or strips
11. Continuous band of windows
12. Flanking wings
13. Central block
14. Casement-type window with leaded panes or lights in geometric patterns

A. Robie House, Chicago, Illinois
B. Brookfield Kindergarten, Brookfield, Illinois
C. Windows, Robie House, Chicago, Illinois
D. Steffens House, Chicago, Illinois

The Prairie Style takes its name from the prairies of the Midwest, where the style was generated and the best examples were built. Its low horizontal lines and projecting eaves are said to reflect the broad expanses of the prairie, though many examples were built on tiny urban lots. The Prairie Style was developed by Frank Lloyd Wright and other Chicago area architects, though the genius of Wright's work, as exemplified by the windows of the Robie House, outshines the rest.

International Style 1920–1945

The International style is characterized by flat roof tops, smooth and uniform wall surface, large expanse of windows, and projecting or cantilevered balconies and upper floor. The complete absence of ornamentation also is typical. The asymmetrically balanced composition is at times placed in a dramatic context or orientation with the landscape. Projecting eaves are closed or boxed and covered with the same finish as the wall surface. Roofs without eaves terminate flush with the plane of the wall. Wood and metal casement windows set flush to the wall as well as sliding windows are popular. A series of small rectangular windows often are placed high up along the wall surface forming a clerestory. Some permanently closed or fixed windows extend from floor to ceiling in a single pane creating large curtain-like walls of glass. Wooden trim is often painted or stained in earth tones to contrast with the white painted board siding or plastered surface.

1. **Plain stucco or plaster surface**
2. **Metal casement windows**
3. **Absence of cornice or projecting eaves**
4. **Curtain wall of glass**
5. **Cantilevered balcony or upper floor**
6. **Closed or boxed eaves**
7. **Clerestory windows**

A. Lovell House, Los Angeles, California
B. Philadelphia Savings Fund Society Building, Philadelphia, Pennsylvania
The International Style was not widely accepted in America before World War II. The two buildings shown here illustrate residential and commercial applications of the style and two of the very few prewar examples in America.

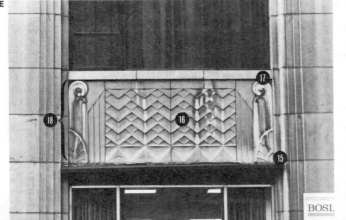

Art Deco   1925–1940

Art Deco is characterized by a linear, hard edge or angular composition often with a vertical emphasis and highlighted with stylized decoration. The facades of buildings often are arranged in a series of set backs emphasizing the geometric form. Strips of windows with decorated spandrels add to the vertical feeling of the composition. Hard-edged low relief ornamentation is found around door and window openings, string courses and along the roof edges or parapet. Ornamental detailing often is executed in the same material as the building or in various metals, colored glazed bricks or mosaic tiles. Although straight-headed windows (metal sash or casement type) are more popular, an occasional circular window or rounded window and door jamb is found.

1. Stepped or set-back facade
2. Stylized figure sculpture
3. Octagonal lamps
4. Sunrise and floriated patterns
5. Polychromatic mosaic tiles
6. Stepped frontispiece
7. Zig-zag decorative band
8. Octagonal clock
9. Iron grille work in spandrel and window surround
10. Zig-zag parapet trim
11. Metal panel
12. Stepped window head
13. Metal sash-type window
14. Metal casement-type window
15. Sunrise
16. Chevron and lozenge molding
17. Volutes
18. Window spandrel

A. Paramount Theater, Oakland, California
B. Old *News Advance* Building, Lynchburg, Virginia
C. Richfield Building, Los Angeles, California
D. Union Station, Omaha, Nebraska
E. Prudential House, 55 York Street, Toronto, Ontario, Canada
This jazzy, ornamented idea of what "modern" buildings should look like was a far cry from the austerity of the International Style and was apparently much easier for most people to accept. There are a good many examples of the style, in spite of the effects of the Depression.

Art Moderne   1930–1945

Soft or rounded corners, flat roofs, smooth wall finish without surface ornamentation, and horizontal bands of windows create a distinctive streamlined or wind-tunnel look which characterizes the Art Moderne style. The streamlined effect is emphasized by the use of curved window glass that wraps around corners. Ornamentation consists of mirrored panels, cement panels, and an occasional metal panel with low relief decoration around doorways and windows. Aluminum and stainless steel often are used for door and window trim, railings and balusters. Metal or wooden doors may have circular windows, large panels of glass or patterns with circular and angular outlines.

1. Mirrored panels
2. Rounded corners
3. Curved glass
4. Ribbon or band of windows with metal frames
5. String course along coping of wall
6. Flat roof
7. Curved canopy
8. Smooth wall finish
9. Cement panel with streamlined moldings

A. Trans-Lux Building, Washington, D.C.
B. Olympia Bowling Alley, Toronto, Ontario, Canada
C. Commercial Building, Bay Street, Toronto, Ontario, Canada
D. Abandoned Gas Station, Lynchburg, Virginia

Unbroken horizontal lines and smooth curves visually distinguish Art Moderne from the more angular Art Deco. The idea of streamlining a stationary building is a bit silly and indicative of the faddish nature of the style. Deco and Moderne were both eclipsed by the International Style after World War II.

Index of terms

This is an index of the numbered **boldface** terms set in lists throughout the book. The references following the terms are to page numbers.

Pictorial Glossary of Terms

The Greek Doric Order

The unique feature of this order is that the fluted shaft of the column does not rest on a base. The ridge formed by the flutes is called the arris and the slightly convex profile of the shaft is the entasis. The frieze of the entablature consists of triglyphs and metopes.

1. **Fluted shaft with arris**
2. **No base**
3. **Capital**
4. **Echinus**
5. **Abacus**
6. **Architrave**
7. **Guttae**
8. **Taenia**
9. **Frieze**
10. **Triglyph**
11. **Metopes**
12. **Mutule blocks**
13. **Raking cornice**
14. **Corona**
15. **Stylobate**
16. **Entasis or bulge of column shaft**

The Ionic Order

The unique feature of this order is the capital consisting of large spiral-like scrolls or volutes. The shaft of the column is fluted and has a flat ridge rather than the arris of the Greek Doric Order. The entablature is usually highlighted with dentils along the cornice. The attic base is often used with this order.

1. **Scroll or volutes**
2. **Egg and dart enrichment**
3. **Abacus**
4. **Architrave**
5. **Torus molding**
6. **Scotia and fillet molding**
7. **Plinth**
8. **Attic base**
9. **Fluted shaft with fillet molding**

The Corinthian Order

The capital of this order is enriched with acanthus leaves and small volutes called caulicoli. The entablature enrichments and various moldings include dentils and modillions along the projecting cornice. Fluted or smooth shafts are taller than the Doric and Ionic Orders and often rest on a pedestal.

1. Base
2. Fluted shaft
3. Capital
4. Column
5. Architrave multiple fascias
6. Frieze
7. Cornice
8. Entablature
9. Modillions
10. Dentils
11. Podium

The Corinthian Capital

1. Acanthus leaves
2. Caulicoli
3. Molded abacus
4. Acanthus flower
5. Shaft of column
6. Astragal
7. Fillet
8. Cavetto
9. Paneled soffit

The Tuscan Order

The Tuscan Order which is the simplest of all the orders is distinguished by unfluted columns, plain entablatures and unadorned capitals and bases. The columns are usually widely spaced and of short proportions. Although the entablature is not enriched, large projecting blocks or brackets may be used to support the projecting cornice.

1. **Plain entablature**
2. **Unadorned capital**
3. **Abacus**
4. **Ovolo molding**
5. **Necking of column**
6. **Astragal molding**
7. **Unfluted column**
8. **Baguette**
9. **Large torus molding**
10. **Plinth**
11. **Unenriched base**
12. **Apophyge**

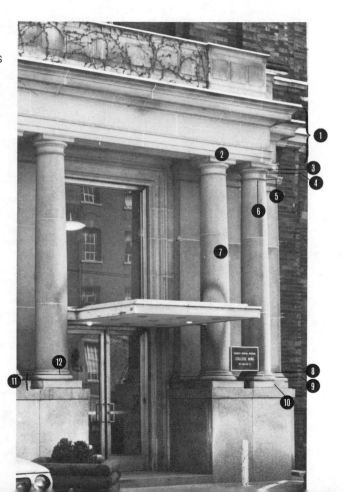

The Roman Doric Order

The column with a base usually distinguishes this order from the Greek Doric. In addition, the shaft of the column may be either fluted or smooth and the entablature may include both metopes and triglyphs as well as dentils. The abacus also is thinner than in the Greek Doric.

1. **Pedestal**
2. **Plinth**
3. **Molded base**
4. **Smooth shaft**
5. **Architrave**
6. **Capital**
7. **Guttae**
8. **Metopes**
9. **Triglyphs**
10. **Cornice**

The Composite Order

The combination of large volutes of the Ionic Order and the foliated forms such as acanthus leaves of the Corinthian decorate the capitals of the Composite Order. The column, often with pedestal and multi-molded bases, has tall proportions. The entablature is large and consists of multiple moldings, various enrichments, and a very pronounced cornice with enriched modillions.

1. Podium
2. Base
3. Fluted shaft
4. Respond
5. Acanthus leaves
6. Volutes
7. Architrave multiple fascias
8. Frieze
9. Dentils
10. Cornice

1. Pediment roof, two slopes of
   gentle pitch
2. Raking cornice
3. Cornice
4. Entablature
5. Modillion blocks
6. Tympanum
7. Lunette

1. Gable roof, two slopes of usually
   the same pitch
2. End wall
3. Gable
4. Ridge
5. Fascia board
6. Soffit
7. Shed roof
8. Eaves

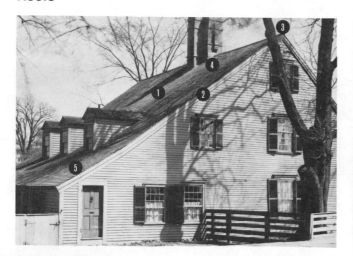

1. Saltbox or catslide roof
2. Rake board
3. Ridge board
4. Wood shingles
5. Shed roof addition

1. Hip roof with flared eaves
2. Hip
3. Valley
4. Hip knob
5. Decorative ridge flashing
6. Slate shingle or tiles

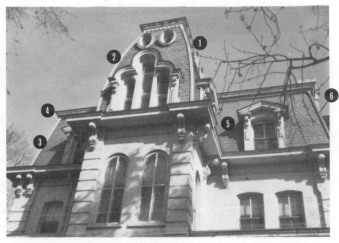

1. Hip roof with large cross gable
2. Gabled carriage porch
3. Hipped dormer
4. Eyelid dormer
5. Simulated thatch roof

1. Mansard roof, four extremely shallow upper slopes and four lower slopes are very steep with various profiles
2. Convex profile
3. Straight sided
4. Curb
5. Hexagonal slate tiles
6. Metal roll flashing

1. **Mansard roof with straight sides**
2. **Cupola with pagoda-like roof**
3. **Fish scale pattern slate tiles**

1. **Jerkin head roof or clipped gable, similar to gable but with gable clipped back**
2. **Boxed cornice**
3. **Crown molding**
4. **Bed molding**
5. **Flemish bond**
6. **Segmental relieving arch**

1. **New England gambrel roof, two upper slopes are steep**
2. **Curb**
3. **Gambrel**

1. **Swedish gambrel, two upper slopes are shallow**
2. **Pent roof**

1. **Dutch gambrel, two upper slopes are short and the lower slopes have a definite bell-like flare**

1. **Rainbow roof, two slopes each having a slight bulge or convex profile**

1. **Tent roof—octagonal base with steeply pitched slopes rising to a peak**

1. **Pyramidal roof—square base with four slopes rising to a peak**

1. **Mansard roof with concave or bell-cast profile**

1. **Hip roof, four slopes with a ridge**

1. **Double hip roof or hip on hip**

1. **Balustraded deck on hip roof**

1. **Frieze**
2. **Bed molding**
3. **Dentils**
4. **Bead and reel**
5. **Scroll-like modillions**
6. **Fascia**
7. **Bead and reel**
8. **Crown molding**
9. **Cornice**

1. Terra cotta tiles and decorative
   brick pattern
2. Molded terra cotta cornice
3. Terra cotta chimney pots

Gothic Revival Roof

1. Curvilinear bargeboards or
   vergeboards
2. Hip knob with finial
3. Pendant
4. Pointed arch or eaves trim

1. Battlements
2. Merlons
3. Crenelles
4. Coping

1. Monitor
2. Full entablature with
   projecting cornice

1. Belvedere
2. Open eaves

1. Octagonal cupola
   with domical roof

Chimneys

1. Projecting wall
   dormers

1. Console, "S" or
   scroll-shaped
   bracket also called
   ancones or corbel

1. Arcaded hyphens
2. Dependencies
3. Central block
4. Interior chimney
5. End-wall chimney

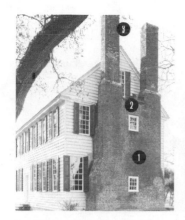

1. Chimney pent
2. Exterior chimneys
3. Stack separate from
   end wall

1. Circular chimney
   pots with battlements
2. Rope-like molding
3. Diamond pattern
4. Octagonal chimney
   pots

1. Circular chimney
   pots
2. Fleur-de-lis pattern
3. Ball and flower

Chimneys

Gables

1. **T shape stacks**
2. **Sloped set-offs or weathering**
3. **Kick**

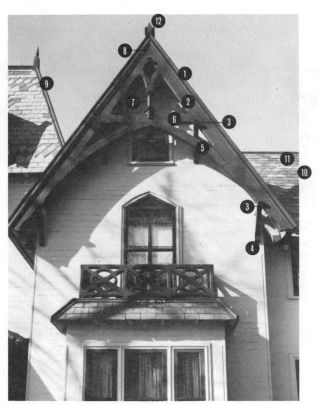

Gable Details

1. Molded rake board
2. Rafters
3. Purlin
4. Braces diagonal
5. Collar brace
6. Collar-tie or beam
7. King post
8. Ridge beam
9. Diamond slate tile
10. Hexagonal slate tile
11. Common lap slate tile
12. Crest-like finial

1. Stepped gable
2. Cartouche
3. Grotesque
4. Volute buttress

1. Bracketed gabled
   overdoor
2. Weather boards

1. Canopy
2. Bay window
3. Cresting
4. Arched double door with glass
   panels

1. Two tier veranda

1. End wall porch or piazza

1. Carriage porch or porte-cochere
2. Balcony

1. Two tier portico
2. Tuscan Order
3. Ionic Order

1. Roman Doric portico

1. Monumental,
   colossal or giant
   portico in the Ionic
   Order

1. Plain 6-panel door
2. Stile
3. Cross rail
4. Bottom rail
5. Top rail
6. Lock rail
7. Sill
8. Architrave trim
9. Broken or swan's neck pediment
10. Pulvinated frieze
11. Fluted pilasters
12. Pedestal
13. Transom
14. Transom bar

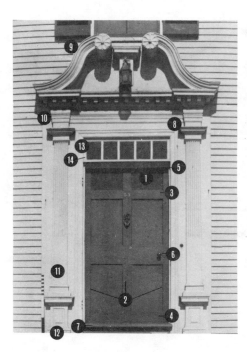

1. Double doors with 4 molded panels
2. Pedimented frontispiece
3. Compound pilasters
4. 20-light sash
5. Cornice window head
6. Clapboard siding

1. Voussoirs
2. Keystone
3. Impost
4. Column or pier
5. Spandrel
6. Abutment
7. Extrados-archivolt molding
8. Intrados-soffit
9. Plinth or base
10. Capital
11. Springer
12. Haunch
13. Crown

1. A pair of vertical panels
2. Anthemions
3. Architrave trim
4. Cornice with dentils
5. Console or brackets enriched with acanthus leaves
6. Sidelights
7. Transom

1. Richardsonian arch
2. Voussoirs
3. Impost return

1. Elliptical arch
2. Fan light with tracery
3. Side light with tracery

1. Tudor arch
2. Label hood mold
3. Label stop

1. Compound pointed
   arched portal
2. Molded archivolts
3. Foliated capitals

1. Compound round
   arched portal
2. Enriched archivolts
3. Grotesques on
   capital
4. Tympanum

1. Rough-sown vertical
   board door
2. Drip board
3. Lintel or head
4. Pintles
5. Strap hinges
6. Jambs

1. Dutch-type door
2. Raised and molded panels
3. Thumb latch
4. Transom bar
5. Transom

1. Molded and paneled
   moveable apron

1. **Sash-type window, 6 over 9 lights**
2. **Architrave trim or surround**
3. **Rails**
4. **Meeting rail**
5. **Stiles**
6. **Muntins**
7. **Three panel shutters**
8. **Shutter holdbacks**
9. **Plain timber sill**
10. **Light or pane**

1. Casement-type window
2. Head
3. Sill
4. Jambs tenoned into mortised
   head and sill
5. Stiles
6. Rails
7. Mullion
8. Quarrels or lights
9. Calmes
10. Saddle bars
11. L hinges
12. Pintles

1. **Triple-hung sash windows**
2. **Pilaster strip**
3. **Pediment roof**

1. **Venetian or Palladian window**
2. **False or blind railing**
3. **Round arch sash**

1. **Two cusp arch or trefoil**
2. **4 cusp arch or cinquefoil**
3. **Cusps**
4. **Lobes**

1. **Rounded horseshoe arch**
2. **Shouldered depressed arch**

1. **Pointed drop arch**
2. **Quatrefoil tracery**
3. **Ogee or inflected arch with trefoil tracery**

Bricks

1. Flemish bond
2. Header and stretcher course
3. Water table
4. Relieving arch
5. Queen's closer, not as wide as a normal header
6. Rubbed or gauged brick
7. Molded brick
8. Glazed headers
9. Tooled or struck joints
10. King's closer, wider than a normal header but not as long as a stretcher

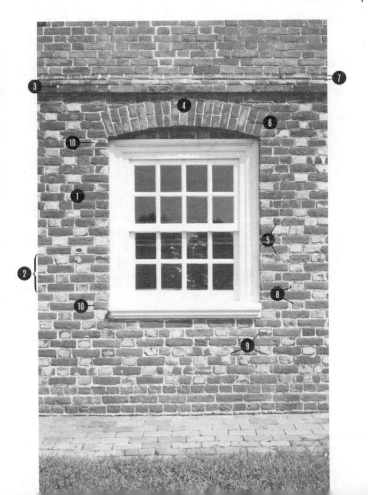

1. English bond
2. Stretcher course
3. Header course

1. Mouse-tooth finish or tumbling of bricks
2. Iron anchor beams

1. Adobe bricks
2. Stucco finish

1. Coursed cobble stone
2. Smooth ashlar quoins
3. Stone lintel
4. Stone sill

1. Coursed ashlar and rubble
2. Mouse toothing or tumbling
3. Brick segmental relieving arch

1. Uncoursed and roughly cut ashlar
2. Quoins
3. Smooth stone lintel
4. Rusticated keystone

1. Random-coursed ashlar
2. Rusticated and coursed ashlar

1. **Rock-faced coursed ashlar**
2. **Rusticated and smooth finished window and door surrounds**

1. **Smooth-faced coursed ashlar**

1. **Uncoursed rubble stone**

1. **Dry-laid coursed rubble stone with small stones and chips acting as infill**

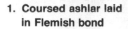

1. Coursed ashlar laid
   in Flemish bond

1. Clapboards
2. Rusticated wood
   blocks as quoins

1. Weatherboard siding

1. Beaded horizontal
   board siding

Terra cotta belt between basement and first floor

11. Base for upper floor

1. **Torus with leaf ornament**
2. **Fillet**
3. **Scotia**
4. **Torus with double guilloche**
5. **Plinth**
6. **Fillet**

12. Cymatium
13. Corona

15. Cornice

14. Bed moldings

7. **Cyma reversa with talon ornament**
8. **Fascia with wave or vitruvian scroll ornament**
9. **Cyma recta with acanthus ornament**
10. **Astragal with bead and reel enrichment**

Bibliography

Andrews, H. Wayne. *Architecture, Ambitions and Americans: A History of American Architecture*. New York: Harper and Bros., 1955.

Banham, Reyner. *The Architecture of the Well-Tempered Environment*. Chicago: University of Chicago Press, 1969.

Braun, Hugh. *An Introduction to English Mediaeval Architecture*. London: Faber and Faber, 1951.

Condit, Carl W. *American Building*. Chicago: University of Chicago Press, 1968.

Dictionary of Architecture. London: Architectural Publication Society of London. 1892.

Early, James. *Romanticism and American Architecture*. New York: A.S. Barnes and Co., 1965.

Evans, Walker. *American Photographs*. New York: The Museum of Modern Art, 1938.

Fitch, James, Marston. *American Building: The Historical Forces That Shapes It*. New York: Schocken Books, 1973.

Fleming, John, et al. *A Dictionary of Architecture*. Baltimore: Penguin Books, 1972.

Gillon, Edmound V., Jr. *Early Illustrations and Views of American Architecture*. New York: Dover Publications, 1971.

Gowans, Alan. *Images of American Living. Philadelphia: J. B. Lippincott Co., 1963*.

Grieff, Constance, ed. *Lost America,* Vol I: *From the Atlantic to the Mississippi*. Princeton: The Pyne Press. 1971. Vol II: *From the Mississippi to the Pacific*. 1972.

Hamlin, Talbot F. *The American Spirit in Architecture*. New Haven: Yale University Press, 1926.

Hamlin, Talbot F. *Greek Revival Architecture in America*. New York: Dover Publications, 1964.

Harris, John, and Jill Lever. *Illustrated Glossary of Architecture, 850–1830*. London: Faber and Faber, 1966.

Hitchcock, Henry-Russell. *Architecture: Nineteenth and Twentieth Centuries*. Baltimore: Penguin Books, 1958.

Hitchcock, Henry-Russell. *The Architecture of H. H. Richardson and his Times*. Cambridge: MIT Press, 1966.

Isham, Norman M. *Glossary of Colonial Architectural Terms*. Boston: The Walpole Society, 1939.

Kimball, Fiske. *American Architecture*. New York: AMS Press, 1970. Reprint of 1928 edition.

Kaufmann, Edgar W., ed. *The Rise of an American Architecture*. New York: Praeger Publishers, 1970.

Maas, John. *The Gingerbread Age*. New York: Bramhall House, 1957.

Maas, John. *The Victorian Home in America*. New York: Hawthorn Books, 1972.

McCoy, Esther. *Five California Architects*. New York: Reinhold Publishers, 1960.

McKee, Harley J. *Introduction to Early American Masonry*. Washington, D.C.: National Trust for Historic Preservation and Columbia University, 1973.

Morrison, Hugh. *Early American Architecture*. New York: Oxford University Press, 1952.

Mumford, Louis. *Sticks and Stones*. New York: Dover Publications, 1955.

Bibliography

Peisch, Mark L. *The Chicago School of Architecture: Early Followers of Sullivan and Wright.* New York: Random House, 1965.

Pierce, James Smith. *From Abacus to Zeus: A Handbook of Art History.* Englewood Cliffs, N.J.: Prentice-Hall, 1968.

Rains, Albert, and Lawrence Henderson. *With Heritage So Rich.* New York: Random House, 1966.

Rempel, John I. *Building With Wood.* Toronto: University of Toronto Press, 1972.

Saylor, Henry H. *Dictionary of Architecture.* New York: John Wiley and Sons, 1952.

Scully, Vincent J., Jr. *The Shingle Style.* New Haven, Conn: Yale University Press, 1955.

Sturgis, Russell. *A Dictionary of Architecture and Building.* New York: Macmillan Co., 1901.

Summerson, John. *The Classical Language of Architecture.* London: Methuen & Co., 1964.

Whiffen, Marcus. *American Architecture Since 1780: A Guide to the Styles,* Cambridge: MIT Press, 1969.

Photograph Credits

Most of the photographs used in this book are courtesy of the Historic American Building Survey, (HABS), and are part of their official records.

Jack E. Boucher, HABS: p. 4 LL; p. 8 UL, LL, LR; p. 12 UL; p. 16 UR; p. 18 LL, UR; p. 20 UL; p. 30 UL, UR, LL; p. 32 UL, LL, LR; p. 36 UL; p. 40 L; p. 44 UL, UR, LL; p. 48 L; p. 50 UR; p. 52 UL; p. 54 L, R; p. 60 R; p. 66 UR; p. 76 UL; p. 87; p. 89 R; p. 91 L; p. 92 R; p. 94 near R; p. 95 middle; p. 97 far L; p. 98 L, middle; p. 99 middle, R; p. 100 R; p. 101 middle, R; p. 102 R; p. 103 middle; p. 106 far R; p. 107 far L, near R; p. 109; p. 110, near R; p. 111; p. 114 far L, near L, far R; p. 115 far L, near R, far R; p. 116.

Cervin Robinson, HABS: p. 16 LL; p. 36 LL; p. 46 UL, UR, LR; p. 60 L; p. 72 UL, LR; p. 88; p. 90 R; p. 93 far L; p. 105 R; p. 107 near R; p. 113 far R.

Ned Goode, HABS: p. 28 UL; p. 34 UR; p. 36 LR; p. 82; p. 103 R.

Arthur O. Haskell, HABS: p. 18 LR; p. 93 far R; p. 97 far R; p. 115 near L.

Lester Jones, HABS: p. 14 top, bottom; p. 22 UR; p. 106 near R.

W. N. Manning, HABS: p. 22 LR; p. 30 LR; p. 34 LR; p. 102 L.

Laurence E. Tilley, HABS: p. 24 LR; p. 38 UL; p. 97 near L; p. 106 near L.

Paul Piaget, HABS: p. 64 UR, LL, LR; p. 107 far R.

Earl Brooks, HABS: p. 93 near L; p. 108; p. 110 far L; p. 114 near R.

Ronald Comedy, HABS: p. 32 UR; p. 53; p. 66 LR; p. 78 UL.

Allen Stross, HABS: p. 42 far L, lower middle; p. 44 LR.

Herbert Wheaton Congdon, HABS: p. 20 LR; p. 26 UR; p. 104 R.

Cortlandt V. D. Hubbard, HABS: p. 10 L; p. 18 UL.

R. A. Mason, HABS: p. 26 LL; p. 113 far R.

Duane Garrett, HABS: p. 28 UR, LR.

Martin Linsey, HABS: p. 42 LR; p. 89 L.

Allen L. Hubbard, HABS: p. 104 L; p. 110 near L.

Fred Mang, Jr.; HABS: p. 2 UR.

Jon Samuelson, HABS: p. 4 UR.

Marvin Rand, HABS: p. 4 UL.

W. Harry Bagby, HABS: p. 12 LR.

Frank Choteau Brown, HABS: p. 16 LR.

Chauncey Buck, HABS: p. 26 LR.

Robert Fulton III, HABS: p. 36 UR.

J. Alexander, HABS: p. 38 LL.

E. P. MacFarland, HABS: p. 38 R.

Conrad C. Stremme, HABS: p. 42 UR.

Charles E. Peterson, HABS: p. 48 UR.

Gerda Peterich, HABS: p. 50 LR.

George A. Eisenman, HABS: p. 52 UR.

Illinois State Historical Library, HABS: p. 52 LL.

Douglas McCleery, HABS: p. 58 LR.

Richard Nickel, HABS: p. 72 UR.

William E. Barrett, HABS: p. 85.

George M. Cushing, HABS: p. 92 L.

Theodore Webb, HABS: p. 95 R.

Theodore F. Dillon, HABS: p. 75; p. 96 L.

Louis Schwartz, HABS: p. 110 far R.

Thomas T. Waterman, HABS: p. 112 L.

Ellis J. Potter, HABS: p. 112 middle.

Properties Pictured

Spanish Colonial: p. 2
    Jose Maria Covarrubias Adobe, location unknown (UL)
    Governor's House, Santa Fe, N.M. (UR)
    Custom House, Monterey, Calif. (LL)
    Mission San Luis Rey, near San Diego, Calif. (LR)
Mission: p. 4
    Santa Fe Railroad Station, San Diego, Calif. (UL)
    Alvarado Hotel, Albuquerque, N.M. (UR)
    2306 Massachusetts Ave., Washington, D.C. (LL)
    Railroad Station, Burlingame, Calif. (LR)
Pueblo: p. 6
    Fine Arts Building, Museum of New Mexico, Santa Fe (L)
    Santa Fe County Court House, Santa Fe, N.M. (UR)
    Southwest Region N.P.S. Office, Santa Fe, N.M. (LR)
Spanish Colonial Revival: p. 8
    McAneeny Howerd House, Palm Beach, Fla. (UL)
    Nebraska Ave., N.W., Washington, D.C. (UR)
    Everglades Club, Palm Beach, Fla. (LL)

    Unidentified Spanish Bungalow, Nashville, Tenn.
    Seaboard Coastline Railroad Station, West Palm Beach, Fla. (LR)
New England Colonial: p. 10
    Jethro Coffin House, Nantucket Island, Mass. (UL)
    Thomas Clemence House, Johnston, R.I. (UR)
    Stanley Whitman House, Farmington, Conn. (LR)
Southern Colonial: p. 12
    Bacon's Castle, Surrey County, Va. (UL, LL)
    Palmer Marsh House, Bath, N.C. (UR)
    Keeling House, Princess Anne County, Va. (LR)
French Colonial: p. 14
    Homeplace Plantation, Hahnville, La. (U)
    Cahokia Courthouse, Cahokia, Ill. (L)
Dutch Colonial: p. 16
    Wyckoff Homestead, Brooklyn, New York (UL)
    Van Nuyse (Ditmas) House, Brooklyn, New York (LL)
    Abraham Yates House, Schenectady, N.Y. (UR)
    Lefferts House, Brooklyn, New York (LR)
    Unidentified Dutch Colonial House, Nashville, Tenn.
Georgian: p. 18
    Belmont Hall (Thomas Collins House) Smyrna, Del. (UL)
    Clivedon, Germantown, Pa. (LL)
    Chase-Redfield House, Randolph Center, Vt. (UR)
    The Lindens, Danvers, Mass. (LR)
Federal: p. 20
    Decatur House, Washington, D.C. (UL)
    Gore Place, Waltham, Mass. (LL)
    Louisburg Square, Beacon Hill, Boston, Mass. (UR)
    Meacham-Ainsworth House, Castleton, Vt. (LR)
Roman Classicism: p. 22
    Framington, Old John Speed Residence, Louisville, Ky. (UL)
    Ridgeway, St. Matthews, Ky. (UR)
    Old State Bank Building, Decatur, Ala. (LR)
Colonial Revival: p. 24
    Wilson House, Pittsburgh, Pa. (L)
    Unidentified house, Manchester, N.H. (UR)
    Stephen O. Metcalf House, Providence, R.I. (LR)
Greek Revival: p. 26
    Joseph R. Jones House, Binghamton, N.Y. (UL)
    Willard Carpenter House, Evansville, Ind. (LL)
    Andalusia, near Philadelphia, Pa. (UR)
    Louis Hammerschmidt House, Monticello, Ill. (LR)
    Tennessee State Capitol, Nashville, Tenn.
Egyptian Revival: p. 28
    Grove Street Cemetery Entrance, New Haven, Conn. (UL)
    Ada Theater, Boise, Idaho (U & LR)
Gothic Revival: p. 30
    Bowen House, Woodstock, Conn. (UL)
    Lyndhurst, Tarrytown, N.Y. (LL)
    James Winslow Gatehouse, Poughkeepsie, N.Y. (UR)
    St. Luke's Episcopal Church, near Cahaba, Ala. (LR)
Victorian Gothic: p. 32
    Newburgh Savings Bank, Newburgh, N.Y. (UL)
    Converse House, Norwich, Conn. (LL)
    Chapel Hall, Gallaudet College, Washington, D.C. (UR)